Other Books by This Author

After Easter
Step into Scripture
A Bible Study of the First Acts of the Apostles

The Christmas Story
Step into Scripture
A Bible Study for Advent

Seder to Sunday
Step into Scripture
A Bible Study for Easter

The Book on Bullies
Break Free in Forty
(40 Minutes or 40 Days)
Includes Forty Devotionals to Fortify Your Soul

The Book on Bullies
How to Handle Them without becoming One of Them

JOHN THE BAPTIZER

STEP INTO SCRIPTURE BIBLE STUDY

FROM THE STEP INTO SCRIPTURE
BIBLE STUDY SERIES

SUSAN K. BOYD

WestBow Press books may be ordered through booksellers or by contacting:

WestBow Press
A Division of Thomas Nelson & Zondervan
1663 Liberty Drive
Bloomington, IN 47403
www.westbowpress.com
844-714-3454

ISBN: 978-1-6642-8639-9 (sc)
ISBN: 978-1-6642-8640-5 (hc)
ISBN: 978-1-6642-8638-2 (e)

Library of Congress Control Number: 2022922825

Print information available on the last page.

WestBow Press rev. date: 01/06/2023

To the reader who wants to meet the one who was designated by Jesus as the greatest man who ever lived (Matthew 11:11). Discover how God used a person who was on the margin of society. A sovereign Creator foreordained and empowered a very unusual man in an extraordinary way.

John the Baptizer prepared the hearts of a nation and beyond and introduced people to Jesus, the Son of God. This Bible study is for the adventurous who will open their Bibles, along with their minds and hearts, and step into the Jordan with John to meet the one and only Messiah.

CONTENTS

PREFACE

Why write a Bible study about John the Baptizer?

I wrote John the Baptizer, the fourth book in the Step into Scripture Bible Study series, because John is one of the most fascinating characters in the New Testament. But he has often been misunderstood, appearing as a wild, ranting fanatic. The movies show him shaking his finger at people and shouting, "Repent, repent!"

Yet in researching John's life and ministry and piecing together Bible references to him, another side of John emerges. He was certainly tough as leather, living outdoors and snacking on locust and honey. He was bold confronting sin even in the highest places. But he was also humble, thoughtful, and proved to be compassionate with some of the most hated people in Israel (Luke 3:12-14).

John had a unique perspective by taking on God's viewpoint. He did this by knowing who he was and why he was here. He understood his mission, and he never craved the attention his entire nation seemed to lavish on him. He stepped forward to do a job and back when it was accomplished. Most of all, he gave God the glory and Jesus the limelight.

Who were John's disciples?

Little information exists about John's disciples. To create an accurate portrayal of a student of John's, verses had to be gathered up and threaded carefully together.

You will step into the pages of your Bible as a disciple of John's and experience the historical period in which you find yourself. Scripture never changes, but studying it with this exciting method might change you.

John, your compass in this story, always points without exception or deviation to the Savior of the world. By stepping into Scripture and then stepping back to today, you will decide what you think and feel about John and, finally, the Lord Jesus himself.

INTRODUCTION

Why would you use this Bible study?

Which of these would you rather attend: first, the most sought-after Broadway play, sitting in complimentary orchestra seats; second, your favorite sporting event in free seats so close you could almost talk to the players; or third, a Bible study? Let's be honest. Attending the first two events, you would be lost in the action and immersed in the details of everything that was happening in front of you.

Bible study should be just as captivating as a Broadway hit and as exciting as a sporting event. Experiencing as well as reading the Bible is the reason the Step into Scripture Bible Study series was created.

This interactive study allows you to insert yourself into Scripture in the middle of the action. You become part of the story. You have the opportunity to interact with biblical figures and respond as events unfold around you. The intention of this study is to make the Bible come alive and the Word of God active in your life.

As you step into the story of John the Baptizer, you do not replace anyone in Scripture, and the Bible verses do not change. You, however, might see Scripture differently after stepping through this hole in time.

How to get the most from this Bible study?

Study *John the Baptizer–Step into Scripture* as your own personal journey with Christ or in a group setting. If you are doing this book with a group, listen to others' points of view as no answer is wrong if based on Scripture. Give everyone an opportunity to share in the discussion. Try to complete the week's lesson before you all meet together.

Do just one or two questions each day. The lesson will mean more if you take personal time to study before coming together to share insights. Application questions are at the end of each lesson.

Each question has verses to help you with your answer. If you, however, want a more in-depth study, look up the chapters and verses under the *Lesson* heading and particularly in the *Scene* and *Note* sections.

The section that is labelled *Scene* sets the stage and helps you picture the setting more vividly. *Note* sections are there for historical background and additional information to give Scriptures a context. *Note* sections are the only sections not written in the present tense.

Pictures are placed at the beginning and ending of each lesson, making the Bible passages more visual for the reader. Poems follow each lesson to reinforce the content in Scripture or as an application for today.

Read the preface, introduction, questions, scenes, notes, and poems together, if you are in a group discussion. This will help you share the experience. *Resist the temptation to skip past any of these!* They are intentional and meant to bring you closer to the action, drama, and truth of Scripture.

Pray before you study each day, and the Lord will give you his perspective. He was there when the events took place and is with you now as you dig into his Word.

Get ready! Scripture is carefully kept in tack, but for the first time in this series, a back story was written about you in the first two chapters in the book, before you interact with John as the Baptizer.

The hope is that you will enjoy and become deeply involved in John's ministry, appreciating the impact he has had on the world. *The ultimate hope* is that you will believe as strongly as John did in Jesus Christ, the Messiah, the Son of God.

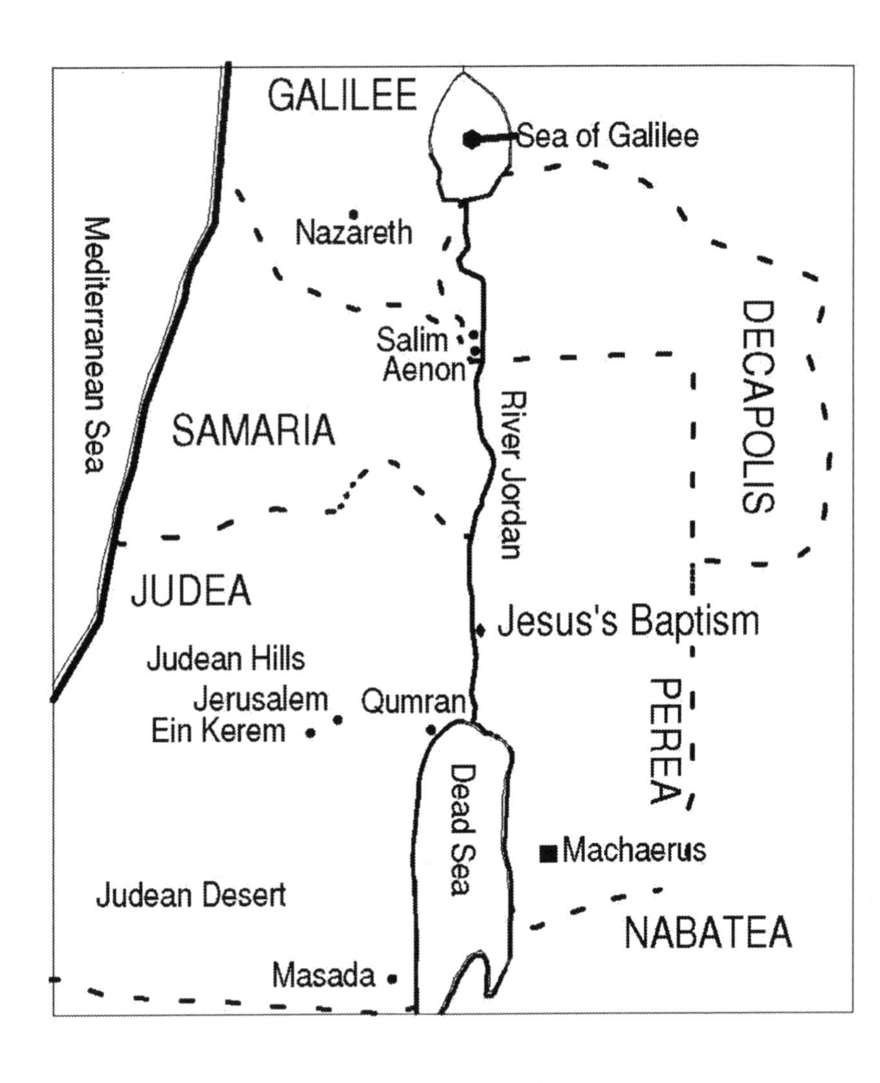

LESSONS

1. Ein Kerem
2. Qumran & R Jordan
3. R Jordan
4. Jesus's Baptism
5. R Jordan
6. Salim by Aenon
7. Machaerus
8. Galilee
9. Machaerus
10. Sea of Galilee
11. Jerusalem
12. Galilee & R Jordan

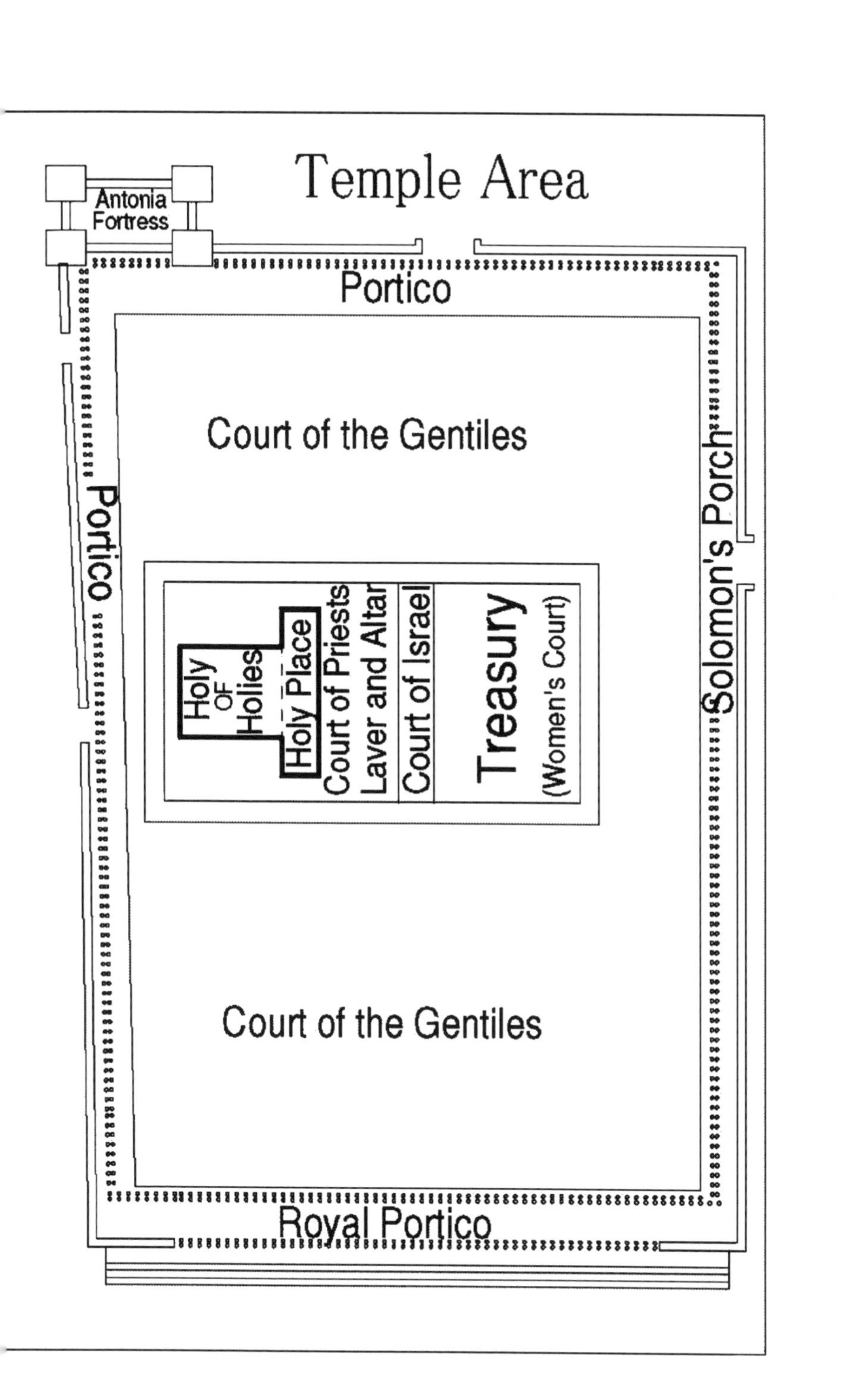
Temple Area
Antonia Fortress
Portico
Court of the Gentiles
Portico
Holy OF Holies
Holy Place
Court of Priests
Laver and Altar
Court of Israel
Treasury
(Women's Court)
Solomon's Porch
Court of the Gentiles
Royal Portico

Cave in Qumran, Israel, where the
Dead Sea Scrolls were found

LESSON 1

JOHN'S BIRTH; GOD'S PLAN

LUKE 1

Note

Almost nothing is known about John's early life. You and your family in this story come from the author's imagination and from yours. John and his family, however, come directly from the pages of the Bible. Chapters and verses are cited so you can follow everything revealed in Scripture.

Scene

Israel is your country. Herod is the tetrarch, and Rome has occupied and controlled your nation for generations. You live in the village of Ein Kerem[1].

At eight years old, you like being acquainted with everyone in the village and knowing that everybody looks out for you. Like most small towns, people are eager to share the most exciting news or even relive events from the past together in re-telling local history (Luke 1:65).

Your favorite story centers on the birth of one of the boys you and many of the other children look up to–John who is twelve years old (Luke 1:14). John seems older than his years. You cannot recall a time when he didn't seem, to you, to be more spiritual than any of the rabbis (Luke 1:15).

John is, in your opinion, as wise as the teachers and as confident as the bravest man in Palestine (Luke 1:16-17)! You watch and listen to him whenever you get the chance. You tell your parents, "No one is like John," and surprisingly, your parents agree (Matthew 11:11).

1. Describe Elizabeth and Zechariah and their situation (Luke 1:5-7).

2. What happened when Zechariah was on duty in the temple (Luke 1:8-12)?

3. What did the angel tell Zechariah about his soon-to-be-son, John (Luke 1: 13-17)?

4. Recount the events that took place after the angel gave Zechariah the news (Luke 1:18-25).

5. Describe some details leading up to Mary's visit with Elizabeth. What was John's reaction in the womb and Elizabeth's response (Luke 1:26-56)?

6. Describe everything the neighbors experienced, saw, and heard when John was born and given his name (Luke 1:57-66)?

7. What did Zechariah, filled with the Holy Spirit, prophesy about God's Son, Jesus (Luke 1:67-75)?

8. What did Zechariah prophesy about his own son, John (Luke 1:76-79)?

9. Step out of Scripture and step back to today for this question. This is a four-part question.

   What did you notice in these passages that impresses you about God's faithfulness to keep his word and fulfill his purpose?

Find Scriptures that remind you that God had a plan for your life even before you were born (Jeremiah 1:5; Psalm 139:16; Ephesians 1:4; Romans 8:29). Choose one to memorize this week.

What is one thing you think God has destined you to do? This can even be a small deed which can make a great difference in other people's lives (Ephesians 1:4).

If you are not sure what you are destined to do, will you pray this week, like Mary, praising God before seeing the result? Are you doubting, as did Zechariah, that God can do something fantastic with you at this time in your life? If so, will you like Zechariah obey God anyway?

Write your prayer here. Prayer is simply talking to God. Have a talk with God by writing your thoughts below.

____

____

____

____

Dead Sea Salt Shore

BORN TO BE YOURS

Lord, you gave purpose to our lives,
Glimpses so we might understand,
We were born to glorify you,
Within your perfect plan.

Jordan River in Bethany. Arabic script on the granite slab.

LESSON 2

JOHN'S LIFESTYLE; PEOPLE'S BAPTISM

MATTHEW 3:1-6; MARK 1:1-8; LUKE 3:1-6; JOHN 1:6-13

Speculation and imagination are used in *scenes* to keep you participating in the story line. This is done only where Scripture is silent. Throughout the following lessons, your character, family, friends, and people you meet come from the author's imagination. They are, however, similar to people living their lives in Israel as they did during this time in history.

Roman occupation, the corruption within the religious aristocracy and those who were betraying their country, such as tax collectors, were ongoing problems during the ministry of Jesus.

The Bible study will help you by acting as a director in the scenes, much as a director on a movie set gives the actors motivation and guidance. You, however, decide what you feel and think and any action you want your character to take as you answer the questions.

Of importance is to know that Jesus, John, and their disciples as described in the Bible remain unchanged and will carefully match the biblical record.

Scene

Rome has occupied Israel as far back as anyone can remember. When you turned nine years old, your family was forced out of your village by Roman soldiers who came to collect inflated taxes your parents could not pay.

You are turning twelve years old today. You are trying not to think back on those hard times but only on the happy memories with your childhood friends and the upcoming holiday.

This is spring when your family will take the yearly trip to Jerusalem for Passover celebration. Thousands of others from all over Israel will be there. This year, however, is special. Now that you are twelve years old, you are, for the first time, permitted to join the men in being taught by some of the most famous rabbis in the land.

Happy to go to Jerusalem, you are, nevertheless, sad missing your neighborhood friends who won't be going with you. You are especially sad knowing you will probably not see John.

You wonder if the young teenager John shared his enthusiasm and knowledge of the old scrolls with the religious teachers when he went for Passover. You can almost imagine him sitting between temple columns, listening and sharing.

Mostly you wish you could be in the temple, learning beside John with his fiery spirit, his unfathomable excitement, and his deep understanding of prophecies regarding the Messiah (Luke 1:66).

Had John studied Scripture from wise Zechariah? John's father, the priest, you imagine was most likely training his son to become a priest someday. You wonder if he learned from his mother, Elizabeth, who also came from the Levitical priestly line. Or maybe John learned from God himself (Luke 1:5-6).

You recently heard that John no longer lives in the village either. You have so many questions in your mind about John: Did Zechariah and Elizabeth die when John was an adolescent? They were very old when he was born (Luke 1:7). The gossip is that John is living in the wilderness (Luke 1:80). How young was he when he ventured out into that harsh desolate area, you wonder?

You can't understand why John would go live in that wild, rocky country by himself, away from everyone. You recall people loved John and everyone was glad to be around him (Luke 1:14, 58). He was so filled with God's Spirit (Luke 1:15; 1:80). You wonder if he joined one of the Essene groups that lived out there.

Note

Many religious sects of Judaism existed in Israel during John's life (4 BC–AD 32). Three of the most prominent religious sects were the Pharisees, the Sadducees, and the Essenes. The Essenes were known for their ascetic—strict self-denial—and separatist lifestyle. One Essene group resided in the community at Khirbet Qumran.

Who were the Qumran?

The Qumran were people who withdrew from society in a community living in the wilderness outside of Jerusalem, in the Judean hills.[1] This was not far from the place where John preached and baptized. The Qumran community intentionally cut themselves off from what they considered a worldly Jerusalem and a worldly temple. They did not agree with the way the temple was being run.[2]

The Qumran, prayed, ate and worked together, and dedicated themselves to making copies of Scripture. These manuscripts were later referred to as the Dead Sea Scrolls, which were copies of multiple books of the Bible, and other writings. The Isaiah Scroll is one of the most famous of the biblical manuscripts copied.[3] John's very existence and blazing ministry were foretold in the book of Isaiah (Isaiah 40:3).

This Qumran community also wrote their own commentaries and apocalyptic beliefs. One book they constructed was a manual of discipline explaining how to join the community and lead a pure life.[4]

The Qumran's careful copying of Scripture resulted in a representative of every book of the Old Testament, except Esther.[5] The scrolls were placed in caves, hidden in sealed clay jars for centuries, until their discovery in 1947. More caves have been discovered with additional finds, including more scrolls, in the decades since. The writings were protected and preserved by the pottery and the arid climate not far from the Dead Sea.

John's ascetic and early separatist lifestyle suggests that he possibly lived with or had some association with this community before beginning his own ministry.

An interesting similarity existed between John and the community at Qumran. Qumran people identified themselves in their documents as being the ones to fulfill Isaiah's prophecy of a voice crying in the wilderness for the repentance of Israel.

The archeologist Randall Price, in his book *The Stones Cry Out: What Archeology Reveals about the Truth of the Bible*, reports that Qumran documents reveal this community believed once they compelled Israel to repent, it would bring in the Messiah. However, they also believed this would lead to the end of Gentile domination and finally restore Israel to its place of glory (4QpPsalm[a] 3:1; IQ Samuel 8:12-16; 9:19-20).[6]

Though John *was that voice in the wilderness* foretold by Isaiah, his mission was not for Israel's glory but for God's glory alone (Matthew 3:2). He would prepare Israel for the Messiah. The Messiah would preach of a very different kind of kingdom than the Qumran community or the nation of Israel expected (John 18:36; Colossians 1:13).

Another similarity between John's ministry and the Qumran's was the significance of water as a sign of spiritual cleansing. Apparently, the Qumran required a ritual cleansing with water similar to the law for Levitical priests.[7]

Excavations show a community existed with an elaborate system of cisterns and an abundance of water at Khirbet Qumran. Daily bathing had a religious ritual attached to it as they believed this identified the importance of keeping the body as well as the soul purified from sin.[8] Interestingly, John chose baptism and water as his way to convey to the people their need for a cleansing of the heart as their preparation for the coming Messiah.

The Qumran community could have very easily been an influence on John, whether he ever lived with them or not. However, the Qumran people did apparently drink wine.[9]

Scripture is clear that John obeyed God's command for him personally to abstain from strong drink (Luke 1:15; Luke 7:33). This is one reason to believe that when

John ventured out into the wilderness, he may have lived an isolated life, keeping company only with God. John, though, was clearly living as an ascetic, separating himself to focus on God, dedicated and undistracted.

Israel's reaction to John is not surprising. The people respected John's leadership and desire to place God as priority. This remained a sharp contrast to a majority of their religious rulers, who seemed preoccupied with indulgence, greed, and self-interest (Matthew 23).

The people of Israel were ready for John. John the Baptizer must have seemed like a breath of fresh air, stepping out of the hills and into their lives bringing nothing with him but the Word of God. *And the child grew and became strong in spirit; and he lived in the wilderness until he appeared publicly to Israel* (Luke 1:80).

Scene

You are now grown and in your twenties. You like living in the bustling city of Jerusalem. It is more exciting than your sleepy little village. The mixture of sights and sounds make life vibrant.

You like hearing wooden wheels roll on stone streets and sellers calling out in the marketplace. You smell the scent of citrus fruits being sold in carts lining the roads. And you find you are curious about rabbis who frequently argue on street corners over theology. If you stand close enough, you can eavesdrop and learn quite a bit about the Torah, the first five books of the Bible.

Enjoyment of your surroundings quickly slips into anger. You watch a soldier demand money from someone who pleads for mercy. The only perpetrator you detest more is the tax collector. He smiles from his tax booth as the frightened people stand in line to pay.

The Romans recruited the tax collector as they always do from your own people. The tax man gets rich because he is allowed to demand any amount of money (Luke 19:1-10). Authorities don't care what is collected as long as they get their revenue.

Tax collectors are thieves and traitors as far as you are concerned. Losing your home to the tax man and watching soldiers force your family out into the street is a day that is burned into your memory.

You quickly walk away and up the steps to the temple area. This is where you feel close to God and far from Rome. Occupying forces have no presence here.

You sit with others in a semicircle at a rabbi's feet inside the giant white marble columns. This area is called Solomon's Colonnade (Solomon's Porch). The rabbi sits down to teach. His voice echoes, ricocheting off the stone pavers and walls of marble, as he reads from the scroll; a prophecy from the book of Isaiah:

> *A voice of one calling: "In the wilderness prepare the way for the Lord; make*

> *straight a highway for our God. Every valley shall be raised up, every mountain and hill made low, the rough ground shall become level, the rugged places a plain. For the glory of the Lord will be revealed, and all people will see it together. For the mouth of the Lord has spoken"* (Isaiah 40:1–5).

Someone asks the rabbi of whom Scripture refers. Instead of answering, he reminds his students that when an important dignitary, such as a king, comes to Jerusalem, a runner goes before him, announcing his arrival. He shouts for people to clear the highway and prepare for his coming. Obstacles are removed from the road making it level and passable. Then the rabbi tells you that this is what the man in Isaiah's prophecy will announce and do in preparation for the Messiah's coming.

You sit for a while and wonder at the rabbi's teaching. As you slowly leave, you go through the court of the Gentiles section of the temple, where money changers sit.

Money changers, with the approval of the high priest emeritus Annas and Caiaphas, his son-in-law, who currently presides as high priest, are, in your opinion, cheating the people. You suspect they trick the families who bring a lamb offering by pretending to find some flaw, and presenting their sheep as a substitute instead, for a cost. You believe they also take advantage of the people traveling here, by demanding a high price for changing foreign currency into Jewish temple currency (Matthew 21:13).

You remember when this outermost courtyard where even non-Jews were allowed, had been a quiet place, where people came to pray. Now your neighbors call it the "Bazaars of Annas."[10] You are sad and disillusioned that your own religious leaders have become as corrupt as tax collectors and Romans.

You move through the crowd, down the steps, and out into the town below. As you are thinking about the rabbi's words, you meet a childhood friend on the street. He is from your old neighborhood in Ein Kerem. You share about friends and family, and he has news about John.

John has become a prophet and is preaching in the Judean hills. You both pause at that statement as no prophet has been heard from in Israel since Malachi.[11] And that was over four hundred years ago (Malachi 4:5-6). John is baptizing people in the Jordan, a baptism of repentance and preparation as he is proclaiming, "The kingdom has come near" (Matthew 3:2).

Your friend tells you John prophesies about "God's Chosen One," which you imagine is another term for Messiah (John 1:34). This title would, no doubt, be less threatening to Rome and might quiet their suspicions that a deliverer is coming. You then ask your friend if he has seen the Messiah. He says he has not. But he shares having met people from all parts of Judea and many from Jerusalem who came to hear John and be baptized by him (Mark 1:5).

You look at each other with excited expressions. You ask how to find John, and he explains he is camped and baptizing in the lower Jordan River, not far from the Dead Sea. Your friend thinks John is smart to preach in the area, where people are traveling. He explains that John is easily seen and heard and his message and popularity are spreading like wildfire.

You are determined to find John the Baptist or as he is also known, John the Baptizer.[12] Jerusalem, through the Judean countryside, to the Jordan River is twenty-one miles apart.[13]

Note: As you answer the questions in the remaining lessons, two through twelve, glean as much information from the following verses as possible rather than simply summarizing a passage. This is where the richness of Scripture is found, and words come to life.

1. As you approach the banks of the Jordan, you finally spot John. What do you see, and what do you hear (Mark 1:4–8)?

John's appearance and lifestyle:

John's words:

The crowds of people: (Where are they coming from and what are they doing?) (Mark 1:5)?

2. Where has John been going, and what has been his purpose (Luke 3:3–6)?

3. How are you feeling, and what are you thinking as you watch all God is doing through your childhood friend?

Note

John's appearance and lifestyle were extreme by any standard of the day. However, understanding living conditions and society's expectations of true prophets might be helpful.

Locust was a staple of the poor in desolate wilderness areas, where little else could be found to eat (Leviticus 11:21). People gathered these insects and cooked them. Honey was also plentiful with the many flowering plants in Israel (Exodus 3:8).

John's woven camel hair covering, worn with a belt, was most likely a garment. This was the costume of prophets, such as Elijah of the Old Testament, though the camel's hair was prickly and probably very uncomfortable (2 Kings 1:8; Zechariah 13:4).

Paintings and movies have depicted John covered in animal skins, but this may not have been accurate. John, undoubtedly, removed the heavy covering, baptizing in a loin cloth and possibly a linen tunic for modesty, until evening, when he would use his prophet's garment again to stay warm.

4. What do you think life had been like for John when he was alone in the wilderness with God, before appearing in public? What do you imagine were the hardships and the blessings?

   Hardships:

   Blessings:

5. Step out of Scripture for the following question and step back to today. It is a three-part question.

   Who was *your* John the Baptist or someone whose faith you admired? How did that person point you to Jesus?

John learned to trust God by spending time alone with him.

This was part of his preparation for a powerful ministry. Where is your secluded place, and when is your private time to talk and listen to God?

How are you different after your own *wilderness time alone* with God?

WILDERNESS FAITH

Lord, no more distractions,
Let my focus be fresh and new.
I'll be more of a help to others,
If I spend more time with you.

LESSON 3

JOHN'S CONFRONTATION WITH SADDUCEES AND PHARISEES; JOHN'S CONVERSATION WITH THE CROWDS, SOLDIERS, AND TAX COLLECTORS

MATTHEW 3:7–12; LUKE 3:7–18

Scene

Late in the afternoon, you approach John and ask to be baptized. As you walk into the river with him, you begin to rethink your life. You know you should release your hatred for the oppressive Romans and betrayal you feel toward tax collectors and the chief religious rulers. You question whether you can.

As you walk up out of the water, you wonder if the Messiah is coming soon. You believe, as many of your patriotic friends do, that the Messiah will deliver you from the Romans. You hope the Messiah will be a savior and leader like Moses or a warrior like King David.

You are excited to explore more about God under John's teaching. He is not political, nor is he part of the religious establishment. John may be the most honest and selfless person you have known. You become John's disciple.

You watch John each day as he wisely counsels those who come to him to repent and be baptized. If you had to describe your teacher's appearance, you would say he looks rough, lean, and sinewy. You are not surprised since you have heard he drinks no wine and he does not even eat bread (Luke 1:15, 7:33).

You wonder how John has sustained such energy eating mostly locust and honey (Matthew 3:4). Secretly, you hope being his disciple does not mean you have the same diet. You learn his disciples follow John's example of fasting often (Matthew 9:14), which you think you can handle. John's skin appears to you to be dark and leathery from the sun. Though he is around thirty years old, he looks much older to you, which is understandable, having spent years living outdoors (Luke 1:36, 56, 80; Luke 3:23).

Regardless of John's striking and somewhat shocking overall look, his words are warm and tender as he speaks of the coming of "God's Chosen One" to his group of students (John 1:34). But he also has a fiery message of repentance that people are willing to hear (John 3:1-6, 10-14).

You look around at the hillsides dotted with people and the eager faces of others approaching the water's edge. Everyone is waiting for a few moments with the Baptizer. You have thought of John and his incredible faith so many times throughout the years. *The boy from your village has become God's man to the nation!*

As the day ends, people travel back home. You sit quietly with John's other disciples overlooking the river, watching the sun set behind the Judean hills. Then John begins to teach more fully about the baptism of repentance and God's forgiveness of sins (Luke 3:2-3).

Twilight slowly turns to evening, the Baptizer, being filled with the Holy Spirit, begins to instruct you tonight by the campfire about *how* you should pray (Luke 11:1). And you listen intently. (Luke 1:14–16; Luke 1:41; Luke 1:80).

Note

Some clarification may be needed at this point to explain the different types of water baptism as recorded in the Bible.

John's Water Baptism

John's baptism was the preparation of a nation for the Messiah's coming. John baptized and led people to repent of their sins. The word, *repent*, as used here means a total change of thinking.[1]

John's purpose was to soften hard hearts as he announced, "Repent for the kingdom of heaven has come near" (Matthew 3:2). Jesus would later teach about the condition of a person's heart, likening it to soil. Only the soft soil was ready to take in the seed so it could grow. In the same way, a person's heart had to be soft enough to receive God's Word, which could then grow in that person's life and be fruitful (Matthew 13:1–24).

Jesus, himself, was, in fact, the living Word—God in the flesh (John 1:1–18). John was smoothing out the hard and crooked places in people's lives so their hearts would be open, ready to accept Jesus and his teaching when he came on the scene.

Christian Water Baptism versus John's Water Baptism in Scripture

Christian water baptism in the Bible was very different from the baptism of John. John's baptism as well as his message were intentionally aimed at the nation of Israel (Luke 1:16–17), though John received

Gentiles who were willing to repent of their sins as well (Luke 3:12–14).

Christian water baptism, however, could not come until Christ came. (The word *Christ* is Greek for the Hebrew word *Messiah.*) Once Christ began his ministry, his disciples administered water baptism in the same Jordan River not far from John, with Jesus overseeing. Jesus, himself, never baptized anyone (John 4:1-2).

The message Jesus preached after his baptism by John and after his forty days of temptation in the wilderness came with the same announcement as John's, *"Repent for the kingdom of heaven has come near"* (Matthew 4:17).

The believer's water baptism in the Bible was administered mostly by the disciples after Jesus resurrected and ascended to heaven. It was done by many, showing faith in Jesus Christ as Savior, who died for their sins and rose again. This water baptism was recorded mainly in the book of Acts and the epistles (Acts 2:41; Acts 8:12, 36–38; Acts 10:47–48; Acts 19:5; Acts 22:16; Romans 6:3-4; 1 Peter 3:21-22).

Scene

The following day, as crowds of people come to be baptized, you look up to see a few men in fine long flowing robes. You recognize these men as the officials from the temple. They report to the high priest regarding any new religious movement or leader in Israel.

Note

The Pharisees and Sadducees had two motives for investigating John: jealousy of John's popularity and fear of Rome's perception that any large gathering could develop into an uprising. If the governor (in this case, Pilate) thought the religious rulers could not control the people, Rome would step in and take control (John 11:48).

1. What do you notice in John's manner and in his message to these men (Matthew 3:7–12)?

2. What point is John trying to make, and why do you think he is so angry (Matthew 3:7–12)?

3. Are you glad John is confronting these leaders, or are you nervous knowing the power they wield? Explain.

4. Step into the future for this question.

   In the next couple of years, Jesus would give a similar warning to Israel's religious leaders. Draw any comparisons you can see in both of their speeches (Luke 13:28; Luke 19:37–40; John 8:54–59).

5. How is John now introducing these educated theologians to the idea and identity of the coming Messiah? What does John prophesy about Jesus (Matthew 3:11–12)?

6. Step into the future for this question.

   Describe how Jesus, after his resurrection and ascension, did, in fact, as prophesied by John, send a baptism of the Holy Spirit and of fire on his disciples (Matthew 3:11; John 14:16; Acts 1:4-5; Acts 2).

Note

Gospel is another word for *the good news.*

7. And with many other words, John exhorted the people and proclaimed the *good news* to them (Luke 3:18). What or who is "*the good news*" (Isaiah 52:7; Isaiah 61:1; Matthew 24:14; Mark 1:1, 15; Luke 4:18; Luke 8:1; Acts 5:42; Acts 8:12, 34-35; Acts 10:36; Acts 20:24; Romans 1:9)?

8. What does John say about himself (Mark 1:7)?

Note

Each of the four gospels give a testimony to the truth of John the Baptizer's message. But Luke shares interesting additional information about the identity of some in the crowd that the other gospels do not mention.

Scene

Your attention is suddenly pulled away from the religious delegation. You are shocked to see in the crowd, tax collectors, and Roman soldiers make their way down to the river's edge. You turn and face them.

9. What do these people ask the Baptizer, and what does he answer (Luke 3:10–14)?

   The crowds (Luke 3:10–11):

The tax collectors (Luke 3:12–13):

The Roman soldiers (Luke 3:14):

10. Why do you imagine John is more receptive to these individuals than he was when addressing the temple delegation?

11. What is your opinion of these soldiers and tax collectors? Describe any conflicting thoughts and feelings you might be having regarding John's gracious counsel to people who could be easily regarded as enemies.

12. Step into the future for this question.

    What are some similarities in the way John prepared people for Jesus and the way Jesus ministered to people (Matthew 7:1–5; Matthew 9:9–13; Matthew 18:21–22; Luke 19:1–10; Luke 23: 32–43)?

13. Step out of Scripture and step back to today for this question. It is a five-part question.

    What are you learning after picturing yourself stepping into Scripture with John?

    List new thoughts or insights you have about John and of the Messiah John proclaimed.

    Your insights regarding:

    John

Messiah

John boldly confronted the Sadducees and Pharisees. But he gently communicated and counseled with the crowds, Roman soldiers, and tax collectors.

Which of the following is more difficult for you to do?

- Confront someone who has the power to hurt you—like the religious delegation.
- Counsel gently someone who has wronged you or others—like the tax collectors and Roman soldiers.

Which would you like the Holy Spirit to develop in you: a softer heart or a bolder spirit? Or both? Explain your answer.

Tell the Lord about it. Write your prayer below:

____

____

____

____

____

____

____

Green waters by the River Jordan in Eastern Israel

THE RIVERBANK

I don't want to be a Sadducee,
Who stands on a hill looking down,
Watching the action of God at work,
While I judge, criticize–frown.

I want to be a soldier with a conscience,
Asking, "What now should I do?"
Lord, give me a heart that cares
About others because of you.

If I have been like that tax collector,
Lord, help me change my mind
To repent of my greed and know what I need,
To be fair, generous–kind.

Mostly I want to have the courage
To step off the spectator shore,
And get my feet wet and never forget,
A new life lies ahead with you, Lord.

LESSON 4

JESUS'S BAPTISM BY JOHN

MATTHEW 3:13–17; MARK 1:9–11; LUKE 3:21–23; JOHN 1:29–34

Scene

Weeks have gone by. This afternoon seems like any other day; you are assisting John now that you are one of his disciples. Lots of people are still coming to the Jordan, looking for the Baptizer. But while the crowds move around and others are being baptized, you notice something unusual (Luke 3:21).

John looks awestruck as he peers into the face of a man standing in the water next to him. People typically ask John questions as they request baptism. John, however, is the one asking the questions now. You wonder if the two men are related as you believe you see a family resemblance between them.

1. Who is this person, and from where has he come (Matthew 3:13; Mark 1:9; Luke 3:15-16; John 1:1-18)?

2. What does John mean by "He who comes after me has surpassed me because he was before me" (John 1:1-5, 15)?

Note

Though Jesus and John were relatives, this may have been the first they saw each other face-to-face. John testified, "I myself did not know him, but the reason I came baptizing with water was that he might be revealed to Israel" (John 1:31).

Surely Mary and Elizabeth shared the circumstances surrounding their own pregnancies with their sons at some point. They must have included the boys' first meeting; John, filled with the Holy Spirit, leaped in his mother's womb as Mary drew near, probably bearing Jesus in her womb (Luke 1:41).

The boys were, no doubt, told the information the angel proclaimed about their own futures. What parent would keep that knowledge from a son when God saw fit to reveal it? Even so, the boys may have been kept apart all those years.

John knew of Jesus, of course. John must have wanted to leap once again when he realized Jesus stood before him. The day John baptized him, John saw in person "God's Chosen One," of whom he had been proclaiming all along (John 1:34).

God himself would be the one to finally confirm Jesus's identity to John. John testified God had told him, "*The man on whom you see the Spirit come down and remain is the one who will baptize with the Holy Spirit*" (John 1:33).

3. You slowly move through the water, close to them, hoping to catch something of their conversation. What do you hear John asking Jesus, and what is his reply (Matthew 3:13-14)?

4. Describe the humbleness you recognize in Jesus before his baptism and in John before he baptizes Christ (Matthew 3:13-15).

5. Jesus has no sin to confess. He is without sin. What do you imagine he might mean when he says, "*Let it be so now; it is proper for us to do this to fulfill all righteousness*" (Mathew 3:15)?

Note

Jesus came to earth; the sinless who became sin for the world crucified as the sacrifice in the sinner's place (Romans 5:8; 2 Corinthians 5:21; Hebrews 9:14; 1 Peter 3:18).

In the Jordan that day, Jesus identified himself with all the others in the river, just as later he would mingle and eat with tax collectors and sinners (Luke 15:1-32). Religious rulers would criticize Jesus continually for those associations (Mark 2:16-17). *His* was the true righteousness (Romans 10:4; 1 Peter 2:24).

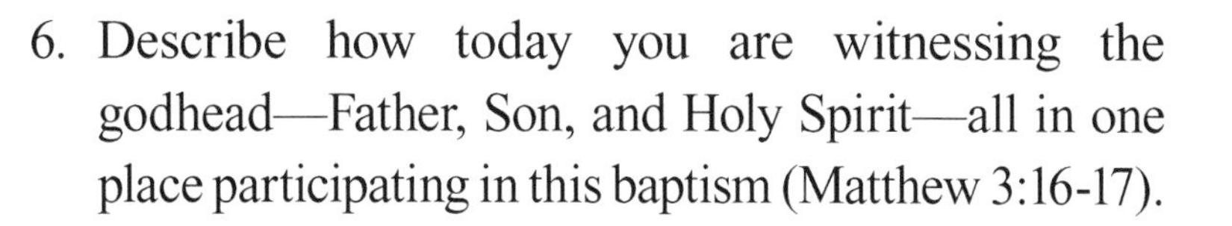

6. Describe how today you are witnessing the godhead—Father, Son, and Holy Spirit—all in one place participating in this baptism (Matthew 3:16-17).

   Jesus, the Son's baptism:

   The Holy Spirit's appearance:

   The Father's voice and action from heaven:

Note

Who is the Trinity?

The term *trinity* is God–three in one: Father, Son, and Holy Spirit.

The first time that Scripture records the Father, Son, and Holy Spirit working together was in the creation story. All three were actively involved: *In the beginning God created the heavens and the earth. Now the earth was formless and empty, darkness was over the surface of the deep, and the Spirit of God was hovering over the waters* (Genesis 1:1-2). *Then God said, "Let us make man in our image, in our likeness …* (Genesis 1:26).

The "*our*" in Genesis 1:26 seems to be the Father speaking to the preincarnate Son (Jesus before he was in the flesh), contemplating and deciding to create human beings made in God's likeness. Other New Testament Scriptures support this (John 6:46; John 10:30; John 14:9-11; Colossians 1:15-17).

Jesus was there before the beginning of time with the Father and the Spirit: *In the beginning was the Word, and the Word was with God, and the Word was God. He was with God in the beginning. Through him all things were made. In him was life, and that life was the light of mankind* (John 1:1-4).

The Trinity is seen together in the beginning of the ministry of Christ. Jesus was baptized, anointed for an important work for God. The Father tore open heaven and spoke, confirming his pleasure with his own Son, and the Holy Spirit descended upon Jesus, revealing the divine power and blessing for the work of salvation. This was witnessed by John and perhaps by others in the Jordan River (John 1:32-34).

7. What are you thinking and feeling as you witness all this? Are you questioning in your mind whether that which you are hearing and seeing is real, or are you recognizing this as proof Jesus is the Son of God?

8. Explain which part of this baptism of Christ is most exciting as it unfolds in front of you? Why?

9. When is heaven being torn open (Mark 1:10)?

10. How old is Jesus as he begins his ministry (Luke 3:23)?

11. Step out of Scripture and step back to today for this question. This is a four-part question.

    What new beginning would you like to have with Christ today?

    How is stepping into Scripture helping you see Jesus face-to-face, so to speak?

    How did the events surrounding the baptism of Jesus, God's only Son, show the love that exists between the godhead, the three in one—Father, Son, and Holy Spirit?

As Jesus came out of the water, the Father pronounced from heaven, *"This is my Son whom I love; with him I am well pleased"* (Matthew 3:17). What would you like to hear God the Father someday say about you?

At baptismal site, River Jordan, Israel

THE BEGINNING

(GENESIS 1:1-2, 26; MATTHEW 3:16-17)

We saw you wade through water,
Baptized by John who was faithful and true,
Heaven was torn open; the Father spoke,
And the Spirit, like a dove, came to you.

Today was heaven's celebration,
God's anointed work has begun,
Messiah–the Savior of the world,
You kept your promise. You've come!

LESSON 5

JOHN'S WITNESS REGARDING JESUS—THE TRUE LIGHT; JOHN'S CONVERSATION WITH THE SECOND DELEGATION OF PRIESTS, LEVITES, AND PHARISEES

JOHN 1:1-28

1. Who sent John the Baptizer and why (John 1:6–8)?

2. Identify and describe in detail the person who is *the true light* of John's testimony (John 1: 9–18).

3. Step back in time for this question. What did the prophet Isaiah, hundreds of years earlier, prophesy about Jesus, the true light?

   Isaiah 9:2______________________________

   Isaiah 42:6_____________________________

   Isaiah 49:6-7___________________________[1]

4. Step forward in time for this question. How will Jesus describe himself as the light?

   Matthew 4:12–16:________________________

   John 8:12: ______________________________

   John 12:35–36: __________________________

Note

John's gospel records a second council coming from Jerusalem to question John the Baptizer. This may have been a different group from the one described in Matthew's and Luke's accounts.

The Baptizer seemed more receptive to this second delegation. His response was much softer. He did not call them snakes, nor did he accuse them of anything. He appeared to stay more engaged in conversation with these men.

The *Baker's Harmony of the Gospels* places this event in John's gospel account after the baptism of Christ and after Jesus had been tempted in the wilderness by the devil for forty days.[2]

Why the difference in the Baptizer's response to this second delegation? Perhaps John heard more sincerity in their questioning. Priests were also in this group, and John's own father, Zechariah, at one time had been one of them (Luke 1:5-10). John seemed to recognize who was earnest and who was there with ulterior motives.

5. What three groups of religious leaders are talking with John (John 1:19, 24)?

6. Which religious leaders came in the first delegation but are missing in the second (Matthew 3:7)?

Note

Who were the Sadducees?

Sadducees apparently showed up in the first commission only. They were the old aristocrats of the religious leadership. Most of them were related to and appointed by the corrupt high priest. Many were wealthy landowners.[3] They believed only in the first five books of the Bible and denied the resurrection of the dead.[4] They wielded power in Jerusalem and over the religious courts. John, the gospel writer, does not list them as being present in his account.

7. List the first few questions asked of John by these religious leaders and the short answers they get back (John 1:19-21).

Note

Who was Elijah?

Elijah, the prophet to Israel in the Old Testament, never died. Instead, he was taken up by God to heaven alive in a whirlwind, separated from his prophet in training, Elisha, by a chariot of fire (2 Kings 2:11). He was prophesied to return before the Messiah reigns (Malachi 4:1-6). Many similarities can be drawn between John the Baptizer and the prophet Elijah (Matthew 11:13-15).

What were the similarities between Elijah and John the Baptizer?

John was preaching not far from where Elijah had been hundreds of years earlier (1 Kings 17:3). Both men were prominent prophets, appealing to the nation Israel to repent and turn their hearts back to God (1 Kings 18:19-46; Matthew 11:9; Luke 1:17). They were bold in their witness and condemnation of evil leaders who led their nation into sin (1 Kings 18:16-18; Matthew 3:7-10; Matthew 14:3-4).

The two prophets had two very similar female enemies–King Ahab's wife Jezebel tried to hunt down Elijah, and Herod's wife Herodias plotted to kill John. These women were the driving force to have their husbands destroy God's prophets–Elijah and John the Baptizer (1 Kings 19:1-2; 1 Kings 21:25; Mark 6:19, 21-28). Nothing, however, would stop the Lord's plan for these men of God.

The most striking comparison between Elijah, an Old Testament prophet, and John, a New Testament prophet, was the fact that they would precede Christ's arrival.

John appeared suddenly on the scene, announcing the first coming of Jesus, and Elijah is said to come before Christ, possibly at his second coming (Malachi 4:5). Elijah may be one of the two witnesses of Revelation 11:3-12. The Jews expected Elijah to return.[5]

People saw the resemblance of these great men, Elijah and John the Baptizer, and their mission from God (Matthew 16:13-16; John 1:21-23). Christ himself drew attention to their similar purpose and importance (Matthew 17:10-13).

Was John Elijah?

John was not Elijah–his parents were known to be Elizabeth and Zechariah (Luke 1:13). Before John's birth, the angel sent from God told Zechariah who John would be: "*And he will go on before the Lord,* in the spirit and power of Elijah, *to turn the hearts of the parents to the children and the disobedient to the wisdom of the righteous–to make ready a people prepared for the Lord* (Luke 1:17).

8. How does John describe himself and his mission (Isaiah 40:3-5; John 1:23)?

9. What is the final question John is asked, and who is questioning him now (John 1:24-25)?

10. How does John take the attention away from himself and instead highlight the importance of Jesus in his answer (John 1:26-28)?

11. Now that he has baptized Jesus, which words does John strategically choose to let this commission know the *Messiah has, in fact, arrived* (John 1:26-27)?

12. Step out of Scripture and step back to today for this question. It is a three-part question.

What helps you today in your life, hearing the way John answered questions and the way he handled people who were asking them?

How would you like to answer others who want to know who you are in the Lord or what you believe about Jesus?

Did John's attitude impress or inspire you? If so, why?

Faith

ANSWERS

Lord, I don't have all the answers,
So, what would you have me say?
How am I to share my faith in you
In a thoughtful but truthful way?

Then I look at the Baptizer;
He did not know when you would come
Or if you would baptize him instead!
But he knew you were "God's Chosen One."

John gives me such peace of mind,
I can believe yet not fully know,
The closer I am to you, Lord Jesus,
The further my faith will go.

Jordan River, Israel

LESSON 6

JESUS, THE LAMB OF GOD, INCREASES; JOHN, THE FRIEND OF THE BRIDEGROOM, DECREASES

JOHN 1:29-42; JOHN 3:22-36; JOHN 4:1-2

Scene

You are quickly making friends with John's disciples. One in particular who impresses you is Andrew (John 1:40). He is a fisherman by trade. He is in the fishing business with two of his friends, James and John, and his own brother Simon (Luke 5:9-10). But Simon, for some reason, has not decided to come with Andrew to follow John. Though Andrew is John's disciple, he continues in the fishing business with his two friends and his brother. Andrew seems to be a very supportive and loyal individual (Mark 1:16-20).

When the second delegation came questioning John, Jesus had been missing for forty days. No one had seen or heard from him (Luke 4:1-13). So, you were surprised the following day to see Jesus walking toward John. The Baptist saw him too and declared, "Look, the Lamb of God who takes away the sin of the world!" (John 1:29) Then John began to testify to the people coming to him everything that had happened the day he baptized Jesus (John 1:30-34).

Today you are walking with the Baptizer and Andrew and another of John's disciples. Again, you spot Jesus. John abruptly stops and watches him walk by. John turns to the three of you with excitement and announces, "Look, the Lamb of God!" (John 1:35-36) When Andrew and your other friend hear John say this, they follow Jesus (John 1:37).

1. Turning around, Jesus sees them following. What do you hear the three of them say to one another (John 1:38–39)?

2. What do you learn happened later that afternoon (John 1:39)?

3. Who does Andrew take to meet Jesus? And how does Jesus receive this man (John 1:40-42)?

Scene

As days pass, you are missing your friend Andrew. He has been occupied with his fishing business. You wonder how he feels about Jesus after spending time with him.

The stories you hear lead you to believe Andrew's brother Simon (Peter as he is now called by Jesus) may have been impressed with Jesus as well (John 1:40-42). Then you learn about the biggest fish tale you have ever heard. And it involves Andrew, Peter, and their friends, James and John.

4. Read carefully the wonderful events of Christ's second meeting with Peter in its entirety (Luke 5:1-11). As you hear the details of the story of the miraculous catch, *which words of Peter's* convinces you his previous meeting with Jesus had an impact on him (Luke 5: 4–8)?

5. Peter had apparently not become a disciple of John's. Why do you think Peter is now willing to follow Jesus (Luke 5:8-11)?

6. Who else followed Jesus that day (Matthew 4:18-22; Mark 1:16-20; Luke 5:9-11)? (Note: The gospels of Matthew and Mark summarize the calling of the four men, which also includes Andrew, without reference to the great catch.)

Scene

You hear that Andrew has become a disciple of Jesus. You are happy for him. Best of all, Andrew was chosen to be one of the select twelve in the inner circle of trusted students. Peter, James, and John were also selected for that honor (Luke 6:13-16).

Two exciting events have reached your ears. The first happened when Andrew and the other eleven disciples went to a wedding in Canna with Jesus.

Apparently, the wine unexpectedly ran out during the banquet at the wedding. The bride and groom, however, suffered no embarrassment in front of their guests; Jesus, at the request of his mother, Mary, intervened.

Jesus turned large jars of water miraculously into wine before any guest was the wiser. In fact, the wine was so superb that the master of the banquet took the bride and groom aside and told them they had "*saved the best wine until now*" (John 2:1-12). You are moved that Jesus would perform such a miracle for a personal problem and not for public recognition or political gain.

The second event was the best news you have heard in years. Right before Passover, people were bringing sacrificial animals to the temple. Jesus was disgusted watching the thieving money changers and the chaos. Jesus made a whip out of chords and drove all those greedy men out of the temple courts, tipping over their tables.

You laugh imagining the money changers, crooks, crawling on the ground, trying to salvage some of their profits, while sheep were stampeding through the temple, down the steps and out into the streets. You heard Jesus took on his critics who objected to his tactics–handling them as well (John 2:13-25).

You remember the prophecy about this in the old scrolls and wonder if it was written about Jesus: "For zeal for your house consumes me and the insults of those who insult you falls on me" (Psalm 69:9). "Then suddenly the Lord you are seeking will come to his temple. The messenger of the covenant whom you desire will come, says the Lord Almighty" (Malachi 3:1).

News is spreading fast that Jesus cleared the temple. He is more popular every day. He left Jerusalem, and he and his disciples are back in Judea. They are not far from where you and John and his disciples are baptizing people. John has moved north to a different location and is now at Aenon near Salim (John 3:23).

Jesus's disciples are also baptizing people in the Jordan River. You are busy helping John when you hear the sound behind you of angry voices arguing. A man is debating with some of John's disciples about the whole matter of ceremonial washing (John 3:25). Finally, John's disciples approach him.

7. What do you think might be the *real issue* John's disciples are up in arms about besides ceremonial washing (John 3:22-26)?

8. How does John uphold Jesus and his importance (John 3:27-28)?

9. What do you like about the way John views his relationship with Christ and his role as the bridegroom's friend (John 3:29)?

10. Explain the source of joy John is describing and why he has it (John 3:29-30).

11. Why do you think John says, "Christ must become greater and I must become less" (John 3:30-36)?

Note

Some clarification needs to be made to avoid confusion as to why different Bibles will have quotation marks in different places in John 3. Did John the Baptizer stop speaking after verse 30, or did he end at verse 36?

No punctuation was written in the original Greek, so Bible translators had to make these determinations. For instance, the NIV and ESV Bibles have the quotation marks after verse 30. The NKJV, AMP, and CPVD Bibles have the quotations at the end of verse 36. And some versions use no quotations at all, like the ASV and KJV.

Whether the Baptizer continued talking or the gospel writer began writing, the importance of these verses remains the same. John's witness and the gospel writer's testimony continue to point to the true identity of Jesus as God's Son.

12. Step out of Scripture and step back to today for this question. This is a two-part question.

    Name different ways you can point people to Christ.

What do you think is the key to having John's amazing desire to *become less important so Christ can become more important*?

How would you like to apply John's attitude to your own life?

JUST ANOTHER FRIEND OF THE BRIDEGROOM

(JOHN 3:27-30)

I'm learning from the Baptizer;
The joy of being Christ's friend,
Preparing a path and the way for others
So people can come to him.

I don't have the fire of Elijah,
Nor the discipline of John.
I'm not a prophet nor of great acclaim,
But I have someone I lean upon.

He is the Savior who loves me
And believes I have something to give,
I'll take the hand of one who wants Jesus
And gently place it in his.

If I'm a friend of the bridegroom,
I'll rejoice when he finds his bride,
Being less feels best, so he can be more,
In another person's life.

LESSON 7

JOHN'S ARREST

LUKE 3:19-20; MATTHEW 14:3-5; MATTHEW 11:1-6; LUKE 7:1-23

Scene

You have more respect for John, day by the day. Detecting no jealousy in your teacher toward Jesus, you stand amazed. However, not all of John's disciples feel this way. The Baptizer is clear that Jesus needs to increase and he must decrease. John demonstrates great humility. Some of his other disciples, however, are confused and possibly frustrated by this.

You wince recalling the dismissive way some of John's indignant disciples referred to Jesus. "*Rabbi, the man that was with you on the other side of the Jordan– the one you testified about–look he is baptizing, and everyone is going to him*" (John 3:26). Now you hear that some of them actually approached Jesus and challenged him, "*How is it that we and the Pharisees fast often, but your disciples do not fast?*" (Matthew 9:14)

John has been encouraging you and others to move your allegiance to Jesus.

While you are contemplating all this as the days go by, you notice John has taken on a new mission.

1. What exactly is John saying which makes Herod nervous? Why is John being arrested (Luke 3: 19-20)?

2. Had John preached against Herod publicly, or did he confront the tetrarch in person or both? What do you hear, and what do you know (Matthew 14:3-4; Mark 6:18)?

3. John has a stellar reputation with the people. How is this influencing Herod's decision not to immediately kill John (Matthew 14:5)?

Note

According to Josephus, the Jewish historian, John was imprisoned at the castle Machaerus [Macherus].[1] It was one of numerous strongholds of Herod's father, Herod the Great, built in Palestine.[2] It stood on a hilltop and overlooked the Dead Sea. John was in the prison section of the castle but probably not in the dungeon, which was in the lowest level. He was kept in custody in a place, where his disciples could come visit him (Matthew 11:2-4). He may have been in the lower, northern part of the fortress.[3]

Scene

You are trying to grasp the fact that Herod had John arrested. You can't help John, and so you and John's other disciples wait for a time you are allowed to go and visit him in prison. The gossip is that Herod's new wife, Herodias (previous wife of his brother, Phillip), is the instigator of John's arrest and that she wants him killed. She is not able to accomplish that because Herod himself protects John (Mark 6:17-20).

4. Why is Herod protecting John from Herodias and her murderous plot (Mark 6:20)?

5. As the months go by, you and some of the other disciples decide to follow the crowds and see the work Jesus is doing. But first, you have to find him. How will you know where to look?

6. You locate Jesus. He is surrounded by people all begging him for something. To your shock, you hear the elders asking help for a Roman centurion whose servant is sick. What do you learn about the centurion (Luke 7:1-8)? Explain any thoughts or feelings you are having about this soldier.

7. Why is Jesus amazed with the attitude of this Roman officer (Luke 7:9)?

8. Give the news that reaches you and your friends as to the outcome of the centurion's servant's health (Luke 7:10).

9. Where are you going now, with the crowd of people, as you still try to catch up to Jesus (Luke 7:11)?

10. Describe everything you see and hear there and how you feel about Jesus at this moment (Luke 7:12-17)?

Scene

You and your friends go to the prison level of the fortress Machaerus. When you are finally allowed to see John, you tell him everything you have witnessed Jesus do. John sends you back with a question for Jesus (Luke 7:18-19).

11. What is John's question (Luke 7:20)? Do you think he is struggling with some doubts about Jesus? If so, why do you think he struggles?

12. Describe your meeting with Jesus as you relay John's question (Luke 7:20-23).

13. How does the answer you are to take back to John show the faith Jesus has in him by quoting Isaiah (Isaiah 61:1-2)? Why do you think Jesus does not simply answer John's question with a "yes" or a "no"?

Note

John knew how to be alone. For years, he had no one but God during his wilderness time. But then his ministry began. People had been coming for counsel and baptism; his own disciples listened to his teachings every day. John experienced fellowship. Then he had the honor of baptizing God's only Son and launching him into his own ministry.

Abruptly, John found himself alone again; possibly, he was in prison close to two years. He lived outdoors most of his life. Being trapped inside must have been terribly difficult and very foreign to him. Even so, Christ's words surely brought him hope as if he were saying, "You were not wrong, John!" (Luke 7:21-23)

14. If John is not doubting Jesus is the Messiah, what other reasons might John have for sending his disciples to Jesus with the question, "Are you the one who is to come or should we expect someone else?" (Luke 7:20)

15. Step out of Scripture and step back to today for this question. This is a three-part question.

    Do you ever have times you feel isolated or alone? When?

What questions would you like God to answer?

Jesus lifted John's spirits with a verse from Isaiah. Which Bible verses encourage you in those lonely times, or simply when you have questions? Write these verses below so they are handy whenever you need them.

____

____

____

____

____

____

____

ARE YOU THE ONE?

Thank you, Lord Jesus,
That when we struggle with doubt,
You don't judge or reprimand,
You simply hear us out.

We can ask the questions
To answers we should have known,
For you are listening to our hearts,
Not to our words alone.

Anyone can have faith
When the sun is shining bright,
But when the months drag on,
Faith wears thin in dead of night.

As we listen to your words,
Comfort and calm will come,
We have peace inside, as fears subside,
Yes, *Lord. You are the one!*

Eucalyptus trees in Northern Galilee
on the bank of the Jordan River

LESSON 8

JOHN'S LEGACY

MATTHEW 11:7-19; LUKE 7:22-35

Note

The gospels of Matthew and Luke give the same account of Jesus speaking to the crowd regarding John. But each give some added details the other does not. By viewing them together, a composite picture comes to life.

Scene

After Jesus gives you the message to take back to John, you turn to leave (Luke 7:22-23). Then you overhear Jesus telling the people how he feels about John. Your friends hurry back to Machaerus. But you stay behind. Sitting with the crowd, you think to yourself how often John talked to you about Jesus. Now you have the chance to hear his opinion of John.

1. How does Jesus hold John up to the crowd?

    John's strength of character (Mathew 11:7):

    John's humbleness or humility (Matthew 11:8):

    John's calling as a prophet (Matthew 11:9-10):

    John's integrity (Mathew 11:11):

    John's dangerous job as a prophet (Matthew 11:12-15):

2. In your opinion what is the highest praise Jesus gives John today (Matthew 11:7-15)?

3. Try to explain what you think Jesus means when he says, "Yet whoever is least in the kingdom of heaven is greater than he" (Matthew 11:11). Who are the least?

4. How is Jesus pointing out the fickleness of this generation (Matthew 11:16-19)?

Scene

As you are listening to Jesus, you notice familiar faces of those toward the back of the crowd. You have the strangest feeling you know these men. You look at them intently, trying to remember (Luke 7:30).

Now you recall. You recognize these same men in their religious robes; the last you saw of them they were staring down from the hillside at John as he stood baptizing in the Jordan. They were part of the formal commission sent from the high priest. They came to investigate, more like interrogate, John. You shake your head, remembering none of them put a toe in the water. They showed no interest in what John shared with them (Matthew 3: 7-12).

5. What is the response of the Pharisees to Jesus's words today? Why do they feel this way (Luke 7:30)?

6. Who else is here that you recognize from the River Jordan? What is your opinion of these particular people right now as they show their faith in Jesus and their support for John (Luke 3:10-13; Luke 7:29)?

7. What are you thinking about as you walk back to join John's other disciples and talk with the Baptizer?

8. How do you imagine John will feel when he hears what Jesus is saying about him?

9. Step out of Scripture and step back to today for this question.

   Jesus praised John for who he was in the Lord, pointing out five of his attributes. Which of those five would you like in your own life in the Lord? List any examples of what you hope God will build up in you (Matthew 11:7-16).

Strength of character:

Humility:

Stepping out in the calling God has for you today:

Integrity:

Taking risks for Jesus:

Mountain landscape during sunset. (Slope of Mt. Precipice in autumn, lower Galilee, Israel.)

JOHN'S LEGACY

(MATTHEW 11:11; JOHN 14:12)

Lord, thank you–John was not a reed,
That if leaned upon, he would fold,
Instead, you gave him your strength,
So, he was dependable–bold.

John gave no thought to clothes or food,
These were not on his mind,
Every soul he touched, he cared about,
A softened heart was a precious find!

Lord, the greatest man who ever lived
Prepared the way for you,
And yet you promised the least of us,
Still have a greater work to do!

LESSON 9

JOHN'S DEATH

MATTHEW 14:6-11; MARK 6:17-28

1. What is the grudge Herod's new wife holds against John (Mark 6:18-19)?

2. Why do you think Herod likes to listen to John? What do you imagine they talk about? (Mark 6:18-20)?

3. Make an itemized list of the guests and dignitaries who attend Herod's birthday bash tonight (Mark 6:21).

Note

The Party

Charles Croll, in his book, *John the Baptist*, quotes Josephus describing the Machaerus as "breath-taking in the size and view of the rooms even though it was remote."[1] A recent excavation by the archeologist Gyozo Voros compelled him to believe the guests dined outside at the castle in a peristyle courtyard, which was larger than the inside dining areas.[2] If so, then this is where Salome danced for Herod.

Salome

Salome has been depicted in paintings, plays, and movies down through the years as a sultry woman who sent Herod into a lustful frenzy with her alluring dance, causing him to offer her half of his kingdom. Herod was definitely impressed with his new wife's daughter and glad that her dance pleased his prestigious guests. Someone dancing at royal parties to entertain was a common custom. But Salome was probably not a woman but a young girl.

The Greek word translated to mean a young, prepubescent girl is the same word used in referring to Salome. The king said to the *girl,* "Ask me for anything you want, and I'll give it to you" (Mark 6:22). It is used one other place in the New Testament, referring to Jairus's daughter, the *little girl* who died and was raised by Jesus[3] (Mark 5:23, 41). She was twelve years old (Mark 5:42).

4. Describe all that you imagine is going on at this elaborate birthday party, which could be distorting Herod's better judgment (Mark 6:21-23).

5. Herod is happy with Salome's dance. Who else at the party would Herod notice is also pleased with her (Mark 6:22)?

6. Celebrating as the night draws on, Herod may be somewhat drunk, repeating himself and then becoming louder and more emphatic. How does Herod demonstrate these behaviors in offering his gift to the little girl a second time (Mark 6:23)?

7. Who do you think Herod is trying to impress by this pretense of generosity? Why?

Scene

Herod may imagine a little girl would ask for a child's choice of a gift, perhaps even a pony. Salome runs to ask her mom for gift ideas.

8. How does Herodias see this as her own opportunity (Mark 6:21, 24)?

9. Why do you think Herod is afraid to not follow through on his outrageous promise (Mark 6:25-26)?

10. What is happening as a result of Herodias's crafty behavior and Herod's weak character (Mark 6:27-28)?

11. Explain the reality, however, from God's perspective and possibly John's (Psalm 116:15; John 3:27-30; Acts 7:55-60; 2 Corinthians 5:1-8).

12. Step out of Scripture and step back to today for this question. This is a three-part question.

    Have you ever been or are you now in a situation where you have little or no control?

How do you keep your eyes on God and resist being overwhelmed with your circumstance? List any verses that help you.

Have you, like John, ever found yourself sharing God's Word and love with people whom you suspect would hurt you if they could (Mark 6:20)? How is God helping you care about them?

MY MACHEARUS

When darkness surrounds me,
I'm closed in and alone,
I dream of open spaces
That make me feel at home.

I need to keep my thoughts
Centered, Lord, on you,
And just how far we have come
And all you've helped me through.

When my world disappears,
As it did for John,
Help me speak with the Herods
Until my last breath is gone.

I don't want wasted moments,
You're the God of redeeming time.
A river, a castle–a prison,
The opportunity is mine.

LESSON 10

JOHN'S DISCIPLES; JESUS'S MINISTRY

MATTHEW 14:12-34; MARK 6: 29-53; LUKE 9:10-17; JOHN 6:1-21

Note

Comparing gospel accounts, a clearer picture comes into focus of John's remarkable life work, even after death–compelling others to follow Christ.

William Barclay, in his commentary, *The Gospel of Matthew, Volume 2*, reveals interesting behind-the-scenes information on Herod and how the citizens of Israel viewed Herod's killing of the Baptizer.

> Herod's actions in this case was the beginning of his ruin, and so it was. The result of his seduction of Herodias and his divorce of his own wife, was that (very naturally) Aretas, the father of his wife, and the ruler of the Nabateans, bitterly resented the insult perpetrated against his

> daughter. He made war against Herod, and heavily defeated him. The comment of Josephus is "Some of the Jews thought that the destruction of Herod's army came from God, and that very justly, as a punishment for what he did against John, who was called the Baptist" (Antiquities of the Jews, 18. 5. 2). Herod was in fact only rescued by calling in the power of the Romans to clear things up.[1]

Scene

You and John's other disciples are waiting back at camp when a message comes from Machaerus. The news is not good. And when you hear the details surrounding John's execution, you are all in shock (Matthew 14:6-11; Mark 6:26-28). You knew his death was coming. Still, you wonder, "Can it be true that John is gone?"

Note

John Walvoord, in his book, *Matthew: Thy Kingdom Come,* gives a brief look at the day following John's death. "His sorrowful disciples came, claimed the body which had been thrown out as refuse, and gave it a decent burial."[2]

1. Who is the first person you want to talk to after burying John (Matthew 14:12)?

Note

One question that naturally follows–what happened to John's disciples after John's death? Some Bible commentators view the Acts 19 disciples Paul met and spoke with many years later as disciples of John (Acts 19:1-7).[3] Other Bible scholars believe their comment "John's baptism" meant John's message.[4]

So, did any of John's disciples join Jesus directly following the death of their leader? Scripture is silent regarding this. But based on all John said about Jesus, it is not much of a stretch of the imagination to believe that at least a few of John's disciples became loyal followers of Jesus.

John referred his students to Jesus, "This is the Lamb of God who takes away the sin of the world" (John 1:30). Two of them followed Jesus because of John, one of them being Andrew (John 1:40). After losing their teacher, surely some of John's other students were looking to Jesus as well.

On the other hand, perhaps those in John's circle were afraid to be associated with another famous religious leader, knowing Herod might consider Jesus a threat. After all, John was beloved and second only to Jesus in the eyes of many in Israel.

Another fear factor was the possibility that Herod would be searching for followers of the Baptizer. More than likely, a percentage of those who had been with John blended into the populace to draw less attention to themselves.

However, others who went to share the sad news of the Baptizer's death with Christ possibly stayed (Mathew 14:12). And of those who stayed, a few may have climbed into the boat with Jesus. Though Jesus selected only his twelve to be his inner circle, he had many others he sent out to act on his behalf (Luke 10:1-23).

2. What is Jesus doing as you tell him the sad news about John (Matthew 14:13)?

3. Jesus withdraws to a secluded place possibly to grieve and consult with his Heavenly Father. What other reason compels him to get away and

who else is he taking with him (Mathew 14:12-13; Mark 6:29-32)?

4. Do you want to get into the boat with Jesus and his disciples if invited, or wait and follow with the crowd at some other point in time? Give some reasons why you want to go with Jesus now or why you might want to follow at a little distance later (Matthew 14:12-14; Mark 6:29-31).

5. Whether you boarded Christ's boat or followed the crowd, try to describe the miracle you are experiencing along with the other 4,999 people (Matthew 14:15-21) today. What are you thinking and feeling?

6. This time you get into the boat with the disciples. Why does Jesus insist his twelve disciples sail out away from the crowd immediately? What is his concern, and why do you think he stayed behind to dismiss the crowd (Matthew 14:22-23; John 6: 14-15)?

Scene

Jesus finally has time alone with his Heavenly Father. He climbs up the mountainside this evening to pray (Matthew 14:23). Meanwhile, all night, you and the disciples are rowing against the waves that threaten to capsize you (Matthew 14:24). You are all working hard to get to the other side of this lake. But you are making little progress.

7. What do you think you see coming across the water on top of the white caps moments before dawn? Describe this figure's appearance and your reaction to it (Matthew 14:25-26).

8. How does Jesus encourage you with very few words (Matthew 14:27)?

9. Do you want to step out of the boat in this storm and walk to Jesus on the water with Peter, or stay in the vessel and watch what happens to Peter first (Matthew 14:28-31)? Explain.

10. When exactly does Jesus reach out and catch Peter (Matthew 14:31)? What significance does this have for you?

11. Why does Peter start to sink, and when does the storm calm down (Matthew 14:30-32)?

12. What are all of you doing and saying now (Matthew 14:33-34)? Describe everything you are thinking and feeling.

Scene

You have felt every emotion you can imagine in the last twenty-four hours. You struggled with sorrow over losing your friend John, excitement being at the miracle of the feeding of the five thousand, fear for your life and gratefulness to Jesus for rescuing you. You say to yourself, "Oh, if John could only have seen this!"

John had testified that he heard the Father from heaven at Jesus's baptism say, "*You are my Son whom I love; with you I am well pleased*" (Luke 3:22). Now you realize you had not imagined everything you heard and saw at the river that day as clouds pulled back and God spoke. The Baptizer had told everyone, "The one who comes after me is more powerful than I" (Matthew 3:11). John was right!

13. Step out of Scripture and step back to today for this question. It is a four-part question.

Name a time when you found yourself in a difficult or possibly dangerous situation and you witnessed Jesus coming to your rescue.

What loss have you been grieving in your life? This might be the loss of people you love, opportunities you missed, or regrets of the past.

Write these in a simple prayer and follow the example of John's disciples–bring your troubles to Jesus (Matthew 14:12). *Cast all your anxiety on him for he cares for you* (1 Peter 5:7).

When have you seen God work miracles that are exciting surprises, even though you still feel sadness over your personal losses at times?

How is your study of John the Baptizer pointing you, personally, to God's only Son, Jesus?

ABOVE WHITE CAPS

(MATTHEW 14:24-34)

Lord, I only see crashing waves,
Lift my eyes to a different view.
Help me see far beyond myself,
Fill my eyes with you!

You aren't concerned with strong winds
Or a dark menacing sky,
All you notice is my struggle
And the sound of my cry.

You come to me in my worse storm,
Only you can remove all fear.
As I go under, you catch me,
We're in the boat! You are here!

Jerusalem dated from the time of Second Temple.

LESSON 11

JESUS OR JOHN—"WHO DO YOU SAY I AM?"

MATTHEW 14: 34-36; MARK 6:12-16; 8:27-30; 11:27-33; LUKE 9:7-9, 18-22

1. Describe everything that takes place after your boat comes to shore at Gennesaret (Matthew 14:34-36). What are your thoughts about these events?

Scene

People are talking about Jesus and all the miraculous deeds he and his disciples are doing. His name is known everywhere in Israel now. John's name has not been forgotten though. The Baptizer's death is fresh in everyone's mind.

2. Who do people think Jesus is (Mark 8:27-28)?

3. How does Jesus make his question personal? What is Peter's answer (Mark 8:29-30)?

4. How is Jesus's fame and Herod's fear fueling Herod's worry over the identity of Jesus (Mark 6:12-16)?

Scene

The jealous religious ruling class are feeling more threatened. The popularity of Jesus is rising. His teachings are well-known now. The religious leaders are eager for a chance to discredit him. Jesus is walking through the temple courts when they publicly confront him.

5. Which leaders are challenging the authority of Jesus? What are they saying (Mark 11:27-28)?

6. How is Jesus turning the question given by the religious rulers back around on them (Mark 11:29-33)?

7. Explain how the words of Jesus support and defend John and his ministry (Mark 11: 29-33).

8. Why do you think Jesus is choosing John as his subject when questioning the religious rulers?

9. What do you like about the way Jesus handles these questions and his critics?

10. Step out of Scripture and step back to today for this question. This is a two-part question.

    Who do you say that Jesus is, for example: a good teacher, a prophet, the Son of God, or someone else?

    What is your relationship to Jesus, for example: close and personal, distant, unsure?

JESUS

WHO IS *HE*?

The greatest question you will ever answer
Will come in words so few,
Not “Who is the Savior of the world?”
But “Who is *He* to you?”

Jordan River in springtime

LESSON 12

JOHN TO JESUS—WHERE TO GO FROM HERE?

MARK 9:30-37; JOHN 10:40-42

Scene

The more time you spend with Jesus, the more in awe you are of him. He is everything John said he would be. His ability to help, heal, and raise people from the dead is beyond comprehension.

Along with Christ's great power, however, is his demonstration of love and humility. You first witnessed this while standing in the Jordan with him and John. He waited for John to baptize him, though John believed he should be baptized by Jesus.

Now today you hear information that you can't understand from Jesus. As you walk together with his disciples, he shares a confidence that stuns and confuses you.

1. What prediction is Jesus making about himself (Mark 9:30-32)?

2. After Jesus shares shocking news regarding his future, some of his disciples begin having an argument they hope he does not hear. Describe this heated debate (Mark 9:33-34).

3. Thinking over the time you have spent with Christ and his disciples and the public's reaction to them, what do you think has prompted the disciple's discussion?

4. Sitting down, Jesus talks with the twelve; you overhear their conversation. Then Jesus calls a child to himself and scoops the little one up in his arms. What lesson or lessons do you think Jesus is

teaching his disciples (Mark 9:35-37)? List some possibilities.

Scene

You are thinking over everything Jesus said when you were all passing through Galilee. You begin questioning in your mind, “Why did Jesus talk to his disciples about being crucified and resurrected in three days? (Mark 9: 31) He raised others, but how could he raise himself if he were dead?”

You are still wondering about this when Jesus takes you and his other disciples to a very familiar place.

5. Where is Jesus taking you today (John 10:40)?

6. What fond memories and meaning does this special place hold for you?

7. How do you feel being in the area where you were baptized by John and where you first laid eyes on Jesus?

Scene

You are camping overlooking the river as you once did with John. You wish he could be here with you to see this.

Jesus decides to stay here for a while (John 10:40). You look up and see all the people streaming down the hillside as they make their way to where Jesus sits to teach.

Finally, everywhere you look, the ground is blanketed with people. More in the distance are coming then sitting down (John 10:41). Everyone is trying to get as close as they can to hear and see what you now believe to be the Messiah or, as John called him, "God's Chosen One" (John 1:33-34).

The air is charged with excitement. Your mind, however, goes back to Jesus's earlier words about himself: "*The Son of Man is going to be delivered into the hands of men. They will kill him and after three days he will rise*" (Mark 9:31). You keep turning these words over in your head.

You are determined to be patient and learn the meaning of the prophetic words Jesus told you about his own future (Mark 9:31).

Today, in this memorable place, you decide you will keep following Jesus. You are no longer looking for the Lord. You have found him. You don't know if the Messiah plans to deliver your nation from Roman oppression. But he has saved you.

Now you begin to notice some conversations. As you listen, you hear people around you are talking about John. They are giving your friend and former teacher the credit he so very much deserves.

Finally, you smile as you hear the satisfying words from every direction. As the people listen to Christ speak, they turn to one another and exclaim, "*Though John never performed a sign, all that John said about this man was true." And in that place, many believed in Jesus* (*John* 10:41-42).

Step out of Scripture and step back to today for these final questions:

8. Has your study of *John the Baptizer–Step into Scripture* made these events more real or meaningful to you? How? Give a few examples from any of the lessons.

9. What did you discover or rediscover in your journey with John the Baptizer?

10. If you have never asked Jesus to be your personal Savior, is that something you would like to do now that you have taken a few steps closer to him in Scripture? If you already enjoy that relationship, are you ready to step even closer as you study the Bible more deeply and talk with Jesus more often each day? If so, write your new commitment in the space below and date it so you can refer to it whenever you want.

My new commitment:

____

____

____

Date:_________________________

View of Ein Avdat, Ein Valley Negev, desert
and semidesert region of Southern Israel

JOHN AND GOD'S CHOSEN ONE

(JOHN 1:34)

John the Baptizer had a mission,
Lord Jesus, he pointed us to you.
His one delight was his God,
Not what he, himself, could do.

John preached about repentance,
And that your kingdom had come!
He was honored to introduce the world,
To God's Chosen One.

John never desired importance,
He left his mark nevertheless,
By turning the hearts of people to you–
With that voice in the wilderness!

AUTHOR'S NOTE

Thank you for choosing *John the Baptizer—Step into Scripture Bible Study*! Writing this study and including you in the scenes was a joy and labor of love for me. I hope you will try the other Bible Studies in this series:

Seder to Sunday—Step into Scripture

The Christmas Story—Step into Scripture

After Easter—Step into Scripture

Look for new Bible studies coming soon from the Step into Scripture Bible Study series.

Order any Bible studies in the series from the website below:

www.sedertosunday.com

The Books on Bullies:

Order them from the website below:

www.thebookonbullies.com

All Bible studies and books can be ordered from:

Your favorite bookseller or bookstore

Or at:

www.barnesandnoble.com

www.amazon.com

My contact information can be found at:

www.susankboydmft.com

ACKNOWLEDGMENTS

I want to give a special thanks to Pastor Luke and Pastor Tracy, who inspire me and have encouraged me. I would like to thank Erica for her grammatical expertise and direction. I am grateful to Judi, Charlie, Marsha, and Connie for their support and letting me bounce ideas off of them regarding this book. I appreciate my amazing and creative husband for drawing up both maps. I thank Shelly for always being so excited with me as we unwrap my first copy of every book.

I would like to thank WestBow, my publisher, for the professionalism and care with which they handle every manuscript I send them. They know what it takes to birth a book. And they have been with me through thick and thin.

Finally, I thank the Lord for his Word. I am grateful for the honor it has been to step into Scripture and the privilege of being able to take others with me.

NOTES

Lesson 1

1. Charles Pfeifer, BD, ThM, PhD, et al, *Wycliff Bible Encyclopedia*, Vol. 1 (Chicago, IL: Moody Press, 1975), 942.

Lesson 2

1. F. F. Bruce, *New Testament History* (New York, London, Toronto, Sydney, Auckland: A Galilee Book: Double Day, 1980), 108.
2. L. Michael White, Professor of Classics and Director of Religious Studies Program, University of Texas at Austin: *Frontline: "From Jesus to Christ: The Essenes and the Dead Sea Scrolls,"* accessed 4/21/22, *pbs.org.*
3. Ibid.
4. Ibid.
5. Randall Price, *The Stones Cry Out: What Archeology Reveals about the Truth of the Bible* (Eugene, Oregon: Harvest House Publishers, 1997), 278.
6. Randal Price, *The Stones Cry Out: What Archeology Reveals about the Truth of the Bible*, 283.
7. F. F. Bruce, *New Testament History*, 108.
8. Ibid
9. F. F. Bruce, *New Testament History*, 109.

10. Edited by Charles F. Pfeiffer and Everett F. Harrison, *The Wycliffe Bible Commentary* (Nashville, Tennessee: The Moody Bible Institute of Chicago, 1968), 966.
11. Matthew Henry, *Concise Commentary on the Whole B*ible (Chicago: Moody Press, 1983), 675.
12. John F. Walvoord and Roy B. Zuck, editors, *The Bible Knowledge Commentary: An Exposition of the Scriptures by Dallas Seminary Faculty, New Testament Edition* (Wheaton: Victor Books, A Division of SP Publications, Inc., 1983), 24.
13. "Distances from Jerusalem," *biblecharts.org.*

Lesson 3

1. Matthew Henry, *Concise Commentary on the Whole Bible*, 675.

Lesson 5

1. F. Walvoord and Roy B. Zuck, editors, *The Bible Knowledge Commentary: An Exposition of the Scriptures by Dallas Seminary Faculty, Old Testament Edition,* 1049.
3. Benjamin Davies, editor, *Baker's Harmony of the Gospels, Synopsis of the Harmony* (Grand Rapids, Michigan: Baker Book House, 1983), III.
3. "A Portrait of Jesus' World Temple Culture, From Jesus to Christ, Pharisees and Sadducees," Michael L. White, Professor of Classics and Director of Religious Studies Program University of Texas at Austin, *Frontline, PBS,* April; 1998, *pbs.org.*
4. Ibid.

5. Charles F. Pfeiffer, Howard Vos, John Rea, *Wycliffe Bible Encyclopedia* (Chicago: Moody Press,1979), 519.

Lesson 7

1. Flavius Josephus, translated by William Whiston, AM, *Josephus, Complete Works* (Grand Rapids, Michigan: 1985), 640.
2. Werner Keller, *The Bible as History* (NY: Bantam Books,1982), 376.
3. Charles Croll, *John the Baptist* (UK: Malcolm Down Publishing Ltd, 2019), 160.

Lesson 9

1. Charles Croll, *John the Baptist,* 173.
2. Charles Croll, *John the Baptist,* 177.
3. Charles Croll, *John the Baptist*, 174-175.

Lesson 10

1. William Barclay, *The Gospel of Matthew, Volume 2* (Philadelphia: The Westminster Press, 1975), 96.
2. John F. Walvoord, Matthew: *Thy Kingdom* Come (Chicago: Moody Press, 1982), 112.
3. John W. Stott, *The Message of Acts* (Nottingham, England: IVP Academic, an imprint of Intervarsity Press, 1990), 303.
4. Rey C. Stedman, *When the Church was Young* (Palo Alto, CA.: Discovery Foundation, 1989), 145.

Map: Jordan River and Surrounding Areas with Matching Lessons, drawn by Jerry L. Boyd, specifically for this Bible study. Portions of the map were inspired by the following maps:

The Bible Knowledge Commentary, New Testament, Walvoord and Zuck, 19.

John the Baptist, Charles Croll, drawn by D. McNeal and D. Negus, 15.

Map: Temple Area, drawn by Jerry L. Boyd, specifically for this Bible study. Portions of the temple area drawing were inspired by the following maps:

A map of the Temple Area, *The Bible Knowledge Commentary, New Testament,* Walvoord and Zuck, 68.

Josephus, Complete Works, Chapter V, A Description of the Temple, translated by William Whiston, 554.

Printed in the United States
by Baker & Taylor Publisher Services